Walt Disney

Terry Barber

ENTERTAINERS

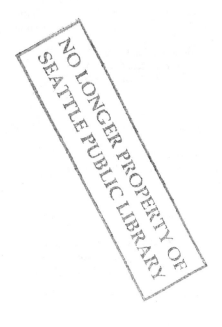

Walt Disney is published by
Grass Roots Press, a division of Literacy Services of Canada Ltd.

www.grassrootsbooks.net

ACKNOWLEDGEMENTS

We acknowledge the financial support of the
Government of Canada for our publishing activities. **Canadä**

Produced with the assistance of
the Government of Alberta through the
Alberta Multimedia Development Fund. *Alberta*

Editor: Dr. Pat Campbell
Image research: Dr. Pat Campbell
Book design: Lara Minja

Library and Archives Canada Cataloguing in Publication

Barber, Terry, date, author
    Walt Disney / Terry Barber.

(Entertainers)

ISBN 978–1–77153–104–7 (softcover)

    1. Readers for new literates. 2. Disney, Walt, 1901-1966. 3. Animators—United States—Biography. 4. Motion picture producers and directors—United States—Biography. 5. Biographies. I. Title.

PE1126.N43B36786 2017   428.6'2   C2017–904626–8

Contents

A group of paperboys in 1910.

The Lesson of Hard Work

Elias Disney hires boys to deliver newspapers. The boys get up at 3:30 a.m. They deliver papers every morning. They deliver papers every evening. The boys work long days. The boys work in wind, snow, rain, and heat.

Boys who deliver newspapers are called paperboys.

A tired paperboy sleeps on the stairs.

The Lesson of Hard Work

Walt is a paperboy. He is only nine years old. Walt is the son of Elias. Walt finds getting up so early hard. He is often tired in school. Walt delivers newspapers for six years. Walt learns about hard work.

Walt is born in 1901.

Walt's mother and father.
1913

The Lesson of Hard Work

Elias wants to keep his customers happy. He teaches Walt not to throw the paper. Elias says: "Take the paper to the front door. Work hard. Give the customer your best." Walt remembers these words.

Elias is a **strict** father.

Walt and his sister, Ruth.
1906

Early Years

Elias does not like big city life. Elias moves his family to a farm. Walt loves farm life. He learns to draw animals. The family works hard to make ends meet. In 1910, Elias gets sick and sells the farm.

Walt draws a horse and sells the drawing for five cents.

These pencils are used to draw.

Early Years

The family moves to Kansas City.
In school, Walt is a below-average
student. But he has a great mind.
Walt spends most of his time in school
drawing. He takes art classes at night.
But Walt knows he will never be a
great artist.

Walt
has three
older brothers
and a younger
sister.

The Red Cross sends Walt to France in 1918.

Early Years

Walt drops out of high school. He wants to join the Army, but he is too young. Walt joins the **Red Cross**. Walt is sent to France. He drives a truck for the Red Cross. In 1919, he returns to the United States.

World War I ends on November 11, 1918.

In 1926, Walt and Roy name their company
Walt Disney Studios.

Walt Disney Studios

In 1923, Walt and his brother Roy start a company. Their company makes cartoons. Lilly works in Walt's office. Lilly and Walt work late one night. Walt kisses Lilly. She blushes. They become husband and wife in 1925.

Walt (on right) with his brother Roy.

Walt Disney Studios

Walt and Roy work as a team. They work as a team for over 40 years. Walt has the ideas. Big ideas cost big money. Roy knows how to get bank loans. The two brothers often argue about money.

These children enjoy a film.

Walt Disney Studios

Walt respects money. But he respects doing a good job even more. Walt wants the customer to feel great after a Disney film. Walt wants the customer to know Disney has done its best. Roy often has to find more money.

Walt draws Mickey Mouse.

Mickey Saves the Day

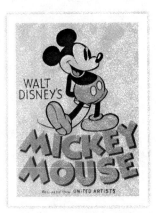

In 1927, the Disney brothers make a bad deal. They lose money. They lose many of their staff. Walt is afraid. The company needs to make money. Walt draws a new character. Walt draws Mickey Mouse. The first Mickey Mouse film is a hit.

Steamboat Willie, the first released Mickey Mouse film, is only eight minutes long.

Walt works long hours.

Mickey Saves the Day

Mickey Mouse is a star. Walt Disney Studios grows. Walt works around the clock. He works too hard. He worries too much. He cannot sleep. Walt has a breakdown in 1931. Walt begins to see there is more to life than work.

Walt and Lilly take a holiday in 1934.

Snow White and the Seven Dwarfs.

The Magic of Disney

Walt Disney Studios begins to make full-length **animated** movies. People see animation as second-rate. But Walt does not agree. Disney's first big hit is *Snow White and the Seven Dwarfs*. This movie shows people the magic of animation.

A *Bambi* poster.
1942

The Magic of Disney

Bambi is made in 1942. *Bambi* is a huge hit. Kids love *Bambi*. Adults love *Bambi*. Walt says Disney makes movies for families. The best movie is the one all the family can enjoy. Disney wants to entertain the family.

Davy Crockett.
1956

The Magic of Disney

Disney also makes many TV shows.
A popular show is *Davy Crockett*.
Davy Crockett spends most of his time
in the wild. Davy Crockett is a hunter.
Davy Crockett is a leader of men.
Boys young and old want to be
Davy Crockett.

Walt works with two cartoon directors.

The Magic of Disney

Every year Walt Disney Studios grows
larger. Disney starts more projects.
Disney must hire more people. Walt
has a good way with people. Walt is
able to see talent. People might not see
their own talents. Walt helps people
tap into their talents.

Walt plays with his daughters Diane (right) and Sharon.

Disneyland

Walt is a family man. He wants a
place where families can have fun
together. Walt decides to build a **theme
park**. Most theme parks are dirty.
Workers in theme parks are rude.
Most theme parks are not for families.

Walt
and Lilly
have two
daughters.

Walt shows a group of men the plans for Disneyland.

Disneyland

Walt plans the world's best theme park. He names the park Disneyland. Walt wants to see families smile when they enter Disneyland. Walt wants to see families smile when they leave Disneyland. Walt wants people to come back.

Disneyland is in Anaheim, California.

People run to the castle entrance
on opening day at Disneyland.

Disneyland

Walt needs money to make Disneyland work. Roy finds the money. Disneyland opens in 1955. In no time, Disneyland is world famous. Disneyland is a must-see for everyone. Real princes go to Disneyland. Real princesses go to Disneyland.

A view of Disneyland from a plane.

Disneyland

Disneyland Park sits on 85 acres. Walt feels Disneyland is too small. He wants a bigger theme park. He wants a better theme park. More land would mean more entertainment.

Today, the Disneyland Resort sits on about 500 acres.

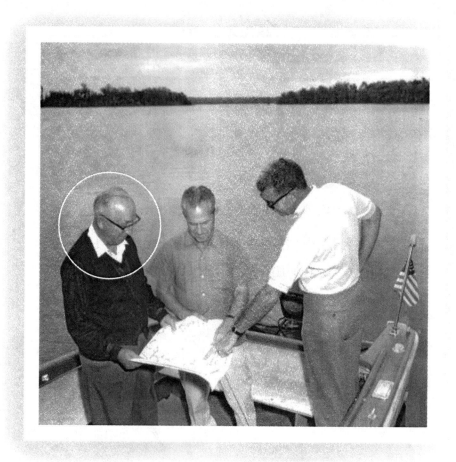

Roy looks at plans for Walt Disney World.

Walt's Dream

Walt wants to build more than a theme park. Walt wants to build the city of tomorrow. He wants a place where people can live and work. Walt finds land in Florida. He plans Walt Disney World.

Walt Disney World sits on 40 square miles of land.

A statue of Walt and Mickey called "Partners."
Magic Kingdom Park, Walt Disney World Resort.

Walt's Dream

Walt Disney dies in 1966. He dies before Walt Disney World opens. Roy works hard to open Walt Disney World. Roy wants to open Walt Disney World for Walt. Walt Disney World opens in 1971. Walt's dream comes true after his death.

About 52 million people visit Walt Disney World Resort every year.

Glossary

animate: to make something, such as a drawing, appear to move.

Red Cross: an organization that takes care of people who are suffering because of a disaster or war.

strict: demanding that rules are obeyed.

theme park: an amusement park such as SeaWorld or Busch Gardens.

Talking About the Book

What did you learn about Walt Disney?

What words would you use to describe Walt?

What did Walt learn from his father?

In your opinion, what type of risks did Walt take to grow The Walt Disney Studios?

Why did Walt have a breakdown in 1931?

Do you think Walt achieved his dream?

How has Walt made the world a better place?

Picture Credits

CPSIA information can be obtained
at www.ICGtesting.com
Printed in the USA
LVOW09s0419040618
579474LV00004B/34/P